The *Heart* of a
Young Immigrant Mother

Rosa Ajanel

Editing help by Stephanie Arroyo

PAGE PUBLISHING, INC.
New York, NY

First originally published by Page Publishing, Inc. 2019

ISBN 978-1-64334-224-5 (Paperback)
ISBN 978-1-64334-225-2 (Digital)

Printed in the United States of America

I can still remember when my parents lived together. Those were beautiful days. To this day, I cannot believe how so many small things were powerful enough to destroy my beautiful family. I couldn't believe that my life changed from one day to another. It was impossible to understand.

My father worked as a farmer and earned very little money. The most he was ever able to earn was five dollars a day. My mom was working, too, but she was only able to earn 2.50 dollars per day. In Guatemala, women's work is paid less than men's. At that time, my grandmother was very sick. She had diabetes, and her medicine was too expensive for my family to be able to afford. My father and mother were not able to buy her all the medicine that she needed because of the little money they earned.

It seemed as if every day, she would need to take a different medicine, and every time we had to go get the new medicine, it became more expensive. My father would often cry because he believed that it was his fault my grandmother suffered from this disease. All this because he could not afford to give her the medical attention she needed.

The jobs in the field are very poorly paid in Guatemala. The pay is even worse for us women because even when we work ten hours a day, they still only pay us two dollars. They will however pay you up to 2.50 dollars if you are an old employee.

Note: Working in the fields is not easy, and not everyone can do it. When you have to survive, however, you will do whatever it takes to get ahead.

There are many types of jobs, but they all pay the same. There are fewer opportunities, and the majority of adolescents do not have the chance to study because of the little money that can be earned there.

Many times, some adolescents take almost six to seven years to finish high school. This is all due to the lack of support and opportunities given to students. These young adults have to work a whole year and save that money in order to study the next year. This continues until they can receive their high school diploma.

Since then, my father have been working in the fields because he never had the opportunity to study because he grew up poor and had to start working when he was six years old.

My father always went to work in the mountains. One day, he arrived in the evening and had been really beaten. He told us that a group of men had followed him and stolen everything he had after severely beating him.

Every time my dad went to his job, these same men followed him. After a couple of weeks had passed, my dad filed a complaint against these people, but the police never did anything to stop them.

This group of people are criminals known as the Mara 18. You can recognize them by the tattoos that they have all over their bodies and the number eighteen on their backs or arms. My father began to fear for his life and ours once these people started calling him by phone to extort him and threaten to kill all my family. He knew that if he gave them what they wanted, they wouldn't hurt our family.

Since then, my family has not left the house, and my grandmother is getting worse because we were unable to bring her medicine.

After all this, one of my cousins disappeared. We were all worried because the last time we had seen her, she had gone to work and never came back.

My uncles had gone to the police to report that she was missing, but the police never did their job to find her. One night, my uncles thought to ask the community to help us find my cousin. That very next day, my whole family had spoken with many people and asked them for help. We divided ourselves into groups of fifteen people and began looking for her everywhere.

It took us a week to find her, but the most painful part about it all was finding her dead. She was found lying in a furrow behind an abandoned house. All my family cried for her because when we found her, she had a rope around her neck, and her body was cut of skin. The pain was especially bad knowing that she was seven months pregnant.

After her death, my whole family was angry and kept asking why the gang had decided to kill my cousin especially because she had not done anything to them.

Afterward, my father told us to stay at home and to not go anywhere. Following that night, my father received a call from those people who had previously followed him. They told him that if he did not give money to them, my cousin's death would have been for nothing. They also told him that if my father would not give them what they wanted, they will kill us too.

Note: There is so much extortion in our country, but our government never does anything to stop these gangs regardless of the murders they commit.

During this time, my father refused to give them money and was thinking about going to the United States. He was worried for our safety, especially after my cousin's death. He did not want my grandmother to keep suffering and especially didn't want to pay the payments to that people who were threatening him.

A few days later, my dad went to a lender. To get the money, he would need to pay a coyote to take him to the United States. For those of you who don't know, coyotes are the people who help pass immigrants into the United States. They charge large amounts of money to take you there.

He obtained the money but had to mortgage the house where we lived. They had given him a month to pay the first interest, which was 8 percent.

After a week of getting the money, my father left. It was the last time I would see him for a long time, and I did not know where he was going. The only thing I knew was that he was running away from the threats of the gang. He thought we would be safer the farther away he was from us.

He embraced us all and told us he was going to return as soon as he could. He promised to my grandmother that not only would she never lack medicine again but that she would be fine and would no longer suffer anymore.

After my father left from our house, our lives became a personal hell. Every night, the gang would come knock on the door of our house. All the while, we were terrified inside. We could not sleep anymore, so my mom talked to all our community and formed a group of patrol men to watch the area.

A couple of nights later, our patrols had a confrontation with the gang that had been threatening us at two in the morning. One of our patrols started yelling and knocking on the neighbor's doors to wake them up. He was letting them know that there were many thieves in town. The whole community woke up from hearing the patrol's voice, and many people started walking onto the streets with sticks and knives that they could use as defense.

Many of that gang had escaped that night. The next day, the people of our town had written a post and put it in the entrance of the town. "Thief found will be killed by community."

Note: The people of a community are what creates strength.

Since then, we have been able to live our lives safely. Although justice could never be done to make up for my cousin's death, we at least knew that nobody else would be killed at the hands of that dangerous gang.

It had been two months since my dad left and had last called my mom. He had called and told her that she had to keep us safe from that gang. He tried to assure her that he would be fine and that she did not need to worry about him. That didn't stop my mom from praying every night. She had a bad feeling about my father's trip, and after that last call, we never heard from him.

My father disappeared, and we did not know anything about him. I remember my mother cried a lot every day, and unfortunately my grandmother had gotten worse. The days passed quickly, and we still did not know anything about him. We lost communication with the people who were going to take him to the United States, and over time, we lost all communication we had to my father.

It had been about five months, and we didn't have any information about my dad. The debt that he had left in Guatemala was growing a lot, and my grandmother was getting worse every day.

Although we were able to work safely without experiencing extortion from the gang that had threatened by father, it was not enough money to cover the debt payments and the medicine for my grandmother.

Note: Going to the mountains and bringing firewood represents the kind of jobs I would do in Guatemala. We would go to the mountains to get firewood and sell the bundle for about one dollar. Although the mountain was far from where we lived, we would oftentimes go about five times a day.

Although I was only eighteen, I knew that I was going to experience a year that would be one of the hardest years of my life. I had a son and had lost my father as he was trying to escape from the gang in my town. Meanwhile, he was thinking about trying to get into the United States for my family. The debt was only getting bigger and bigger due to the interest that had been placed on it. The people to whom my father had borrowed money from were already threatening us because of the time that has passed, and our inability to pay them back. It was becoming very hard for me to live there.

In Guatemala, it's hard to find a good job no matter if you are a professional or not.

Every day, there are less jobs, and with no job and no money, life was getting harder and harder. I decided to go talk to the people to whom we owed money and ended up reaching an agreement. In exchange for paying off every last penny, they agreed to give me a year's worth of time and promised to not do anything to my family.

I thought every night about going to the United States. I didn't want to go, but the poverty was forcing me to leave. And I knew that I needed to find out what had happened with my father. I made the decision to leave to the United States, and every night before I left, I would look at my son slowly and tell him to forgive me for leaving him behind. I did not want to do it, but I didn't have a choice.

Note: When you see your child for the last time and are forced to leave them behind, it's heartbreaking to your soul. You have to try not to look behind because if you do, it is the most intense pain you'll feel in your heart. The pain is so strong that it will break you down.

This was the hardest decision I ever had to make. I decided to leave my son in Guatemala. I made this choice even though I knew that if I left, my son would never recognize me and that I would miss out on all his antics and milestones during his childhood. The one thing I was sure of was that I could not take him with me. The trip would be really dangerous, and I refused to let something happen to him.

I did not want to risk his safety and well-being. I did not want him to suffer during the trip due to lack of food and water, and I especially did not want to risk him being kidnapped by drug dealers like what had happened to my father. I was very afraid for my son.

Even though it would cause my heart the biggest pain imaginable, I preferred to leave my son in Guatemala. He would be safe with my mom. I found comfort in knowing that if something were to happen to me, it would at least only be me. My son would be safe. Knowing that nothing would happen to him is ultimately what gave me the strength to leave.

I did not want my son to grow up in the extreme poverty like I had grown up in. I wanted something better for him and for my family. I did not want them to lack anything anymore, and I wanted to fulfill the promise that my father had made to my grandmother. When I think about my childhood, it was never easy because of how little my family had. I knew I didn't want my son to grow up like that, and I wanted him to be a stronger person than I was. If I stayed in Guatemala, he would not have the same opportunities compared to if I was in the United States. If I was there, I knew he would have everything he needed.

Note: No matter how painful it is to leave a child behind, a mother will always protect her son. When a mother loves her child, she would never risk something happening to them. Sometimes it's more dangerous to leave them behind, and sometimes it's more dangerous to bring them with us. These are hard choices we are forced to make because of where we live.

I talked to a coyote and made a deal with him to take me to the United States. I was ready to face everything and anything that came my way. I had a serious conversation with my family, and it was clear that my mother did not agree with my decision.

She said to me, "It could be really dangerous!"

"I'm going to America. I can't live here anymore. Please understand me!" I said hopelessly.

My mom sadly responded by saying, "I don't want to lose you like I lost your father!"

"The money isn't enough, and I need to pay that debt as soon as possible. I know it is dangerous, Mom!" I yelled loudly.

I was willing to risk my life like my father did. Our needs were much bigger than my fear.

My mother started crying. I kneeled before her and raised my forehead.

I said, "Mom, please do not cry. I'll come back one day!"

"Please do not leave. Do not leave us like your father did. Think about how your son will grow up without you!" she yelled painfully.

"Mom, please don't make this more difficult!" I answered crying.

"I promise that I will find out what happened to my father and figure out if he is still alive or if the drug dealers killed him."

Note: When we make this decision, we feel as if we are heartless people when in reality, this has nothing to do with who we are. We are forced to make this choice in order to survive.

I had to do it for my son. It wasn't his fault that he was born into this world, and it wasn't fair that he had to suffer to survive. He should not have to pay for my mistakes. I do not want him to grow up like I did in poverty. I want him to be a person who can make someone of himself in Guatemala. If I had stayed to live there, I wouldn't have been able to give my family and my son what they needed.

I told my mom that I would be leaving my son with her. I knew that's where he would be safest. I hopelessly yelled for her to understand that I never had a choice.

I couldn't stop crying, but I knew that nothing could change my decision.

My mom slowly started understanding, and we kept talking seriously.

I told her, "Forgive me, Mom. I promise to give you a better life. I don't know when I will return, but I will return. I swear!"

"I believe in you. Your son, one day, will be proud of you. He will understand why you made this decision!" my mom said proudly.

I begged her to promise me that she would take care of my son and never neglect him. With little push, my mom promised to look after him, and I couldn't help but thank my mother for the support she was giving me.

I said goodbye to my mother and my son. I took my son, and I hugged him very hard.

In that moment, it felt as if life was ending. I couldn't help but feel as if part of my heart was staying in Guatemala. The pain in my heart was unimaginable. I leaned down to whisper in his ear and slowly asked him to forgive me and to understand that I didn't have a choice.

I told him, "Forgive me. I will return soon, my love. I promise you!"

I kissed him and tried to be strong with my feelings. My mom gave me her blessing, and I left.

Note: The hug of a child is the strongest force that motivates you to fight for what they need.

A few days later, I found myself on the border of Mexico and Guatemala. The people who were taking me to the United States gave me the opportunity to call my family, and I took advantage of it.

I called my mom, and I heard my son crying and saying, "Mom, where are you?"

After listening to him, I could not contain my tears. I felt miserable and like a mother without feelings, only in my heart and my mind was I saying, *God, forgive me. You know the reason why I left him. Help me. I beg you!*

I began to pray. I felt that it was my only source of strength I had to keep me going.

I calmed down and tried to remove all the memories of my family from my mind, but in my heart, the memories were like wounds, and they were hurting me. I tried not to think about my family, but it was difficult.

Every time we changed cars, I would cry and ask God to give me the strength not to give up and to keep going. Many people tried crossing. There was a hundred of us and most were older. I saw a women who had brought her son with her. He was just one year old. I couldn't help but blame myself when I looked at the little boy. My heart hurt every time I saw him. I could not stand how much my maternal feelings were tearing me up inside.

I felt like the worst mother in the world for having left him.

Every time the pain of leaving him over came me, and I would start to cry, an older man would watch me out of the corner of his eye.

When we were already in Mexico, the old man approached me and said hello in my language. I asked him, "Do we speak the same language?"

"Yes, I speak the same language as you!" he answered me.

He told me that he preferred we speak K'iche so that the coyotes wouldn't understand what we were saying. I knew it was better that the coyotes didn't know I could speak Spanish.

He agreed and started asking me many questions.

He asked me, "I see a lot of sadness and pain in your heart."

I replied, "I feel like the worst person in the world. The worst!"

He replied by telling me, "Sometimes we have to make painful decisions in our lives! We want a better life for our children and family. Do not cry. Do not regret. You did it for a strong cause! Now you are on your way to the United States, close to achieving your goals. Do not let the pain control you and keep you in this painful mindset. Be strong. *God* is always with you to achieve your goals! If you propose that you can do it, you will see that one day, *God* will reward you in the best way."

Note: An elder will always be the best guide for younger generations. They are the people who inspire you to do great things in life.

After that, the older man told me, "Go ahead, girl. You will see that we will arrive in the United States! Just believe in *God*. Everything will be fine!"

Everything, he said, would have been an encouragement for anyone to hear. Since then, I have not cried for my family and son.

I just keep reminding myself that I came to fight for them and find out what happened to my father.

After a few days, they separated us because there was a lot of Mexican patrols.

I never saw the old man again. Every time I prayed, I would beg *God* to bless that old man, wherever he was, and to help him get to the United States.

I was really grateful that he was able to give me such encouraging advice.

Every place we passed was terrible. The cars we were in did not have windows or air conditioning. It was extremely hot inside, and it became very hard to breathe. It felt as if these cars were our graves. The coyotes had deceived us. They had told us that they had paid the drug traffickers so that they would not kidnap us, but it wasn't true.

Note: When I was in the truck, I couldn't breathe well. I remember no one could. But at least these are now nothing but sad memories.

When we arrived to Chiapas, Mexico, we began to make our way to the train. Our destiny included getting us onto the train. The coyotes would make us climb on top of the train's roof so we could get to the border of the United States and Mexico. Unfortunately, the drug traffickers stopped us. They took us all out of the cars and had weapons as big as rifles with masks on their faces. We did not know who they were.

The coyotes negotiated with the drug traffickers and paid a set amount for each person to get on the train. The next day, we were resting in an abandoned house. By dusk, we had been told to get onto the beast. *The Train of Death* as many people call it. They call it this in memory of all the people who died falling from the train or were thrown off and killed by drug and human traffickers.

When I had gotten on the train, it was seven o'clock at night, and I was very afraid.

There were many people coming from various places. Once on top of the train, we set off on the road and did not let our sleep win. If sleep was to beat us, it would mean our death. We tied one foot and one hand to whatever we could on top of the train to keep us from falling off.

Note: We did not care about how dangerous this journey would be. All we knew was that we had to reach our destination.

It was very cold, and there was no food or water. After around three hours on the train had passed, about ten men had climbed on top. We immediately felt that they were a bad presence and were not good people to have onboard. Everyone was bewildered.

The men took out their weapons and began to ask for money from each of us. When I saw them, I untied myself and hid on the side of the train even though we were going at a very fast speed. I had hidden in one of the railings that was located on the side.

I kept repeating, "My God, help me. Please protect me!"

I was very scared, but when I finally looked over my head, I saw them throwing a boy and a man from the train. I felt even more afraid after seeing the cruel act of those people.

I poked my head up again and saw them hitting someone they had caught. Another boy begged them not to throw his friend off the train. "He has a family!" he said.

They just laughed at him mercilessly. They threw him, and I watched as the boy fell to the ground and was passed over by the train.

I was in shock and couldn't breathe from how afraid I was.

Note: This group of former military men are called Los Zetas, and they are an extremely dangerous troop of criminals found in Mexico.

Even though the boy had begged them for his friend's life, it made no difference to them. They really were evil people with no feelings. The men left by the time we had arrived to Tamaulipas, Mexico. I could not stop crying because of what I had seen. I felt as if these men were still following us. I was in disbelief. I couldn't forget it.

Every time I closed my eyes, I remembered those boys. I tried to reassure myself that everything would be okay. Whenever the reflection of the boys would appear in my eyes, I would try to block them out. I kept trying to remember the advice that the old man had given me, and little by little, my fear was disappearing.

After some time, the coyotes picked us up. They took us to a home that was close to the United States. From there, it was only the river that separated Mexico from United States.

That river we had to cross is called Brave River, and we were close, so close. I was grateful to *God*. I knew that the hardest part of the trip was approaching. I would have to cross the river and walk in the desert to reach the United States. The coyotes that brought us to the border sold us to a new group of coyotes that knew the way through the desert and into the United States.

The next day, we left the house in Tamaulipas, Mexico. The new coyotes put us in a small bus without windows and took us to the border. I watched as we approached the river that separates Mexico from the United States. I could not believe how close I was to achieving my dreams.

I wondered where my father had disappeared. I could feel in my heart that he was still alive. I knew I would find him very soon, and I could feel that was close to finding the answers to my questions.

After three hours, we passed the river, but many people couldn't swim, including myself. We had to hold onto each other and make a chain so that the river wouldn't take anyone. After crossing, we were in the desert near where the border wall was. We had to climb on top of the big metal tools that were on the wall and throw ourselves to the other side. That was the moment that we crossed over from Mexico to the United States.

Note: Holding each other's hands gave us enough support so that no current could take any one of us.

We ran as fast as we could. We were now about fifteen people and most were men. Only five women were in our group. Once we jumped, we hid in the bushes under the dry trees so that the US border agents would not see us.

After a while, it was very dark, so we left our hiding places, and the coyotes told us to follow them and move quickly. They were very rude and violent. I did not talk to anyone because I was afraid they would do something to me. The coyotes thought I did not speak Spanish because I would never answer them when they asked me if I had a boyfriend. I would always reply in my language. I feared that they would touch me if they knew I spoke Spanish.

We started walking along the very long road and ended up walking day and night for three days. We were very tired. The coyotes kept saying that we were almost there, but the road would not finish. We ran out of water, and there was no food. The little boy kept crying because it was very cold, and he had no water. I had some water left, so I gave it to his mother for her to give to him. I didn't talk with his mother out of fear of them overhearing me speak in Spanish. In my mind, I couldn't help but think that it was for the best to have left my son with my mother especially after watching how much this little boy was suffering. It was very painful to see him cry.

Note: God said, "Remember that I am always by your side even in the most painful moments of your life."

After another four days, a week had passed of us walking when a man sat down, and a snake bit him. The man told the coyotes to help him because he didn't want to die there in the desert. They took the poison out of his foot, but he was not able to walk anymore. The coyotes turned to him and said, "Those who follow, go on; those that stay here, stay here."

The man started to cry and pleaded with the coyotes not to leave him. A Good Samaritan told them, "We cannot leave him here. He has a family, and he paid you to take him to United States." Another man jumped into the conversation and began to tell the coyotes, "We paid for a safe trip, and you lied to us. We have been walking a lot in the desert and that was not the agreement."

One of the coyotes got very close to the man who was complaining and said, "You do not want to live, right?" Without saying anything else, the coyote shot one of the men, and he died quickly. Nobody spoke out of fear, and everybody stayed quiet.

They said, "Whoever dares to contradict us, you and your words will die like he did. Or worse!" They turned to us and said, "Let's get out of here!" and pushed and pulled us along. All the while, they left the man who had been bitten. He was crying a lot while sitting under a prickly cactus. Nobody said anything for fear of being killed. In that moment, I tried to be very strong and not cry from all the horrible things I had seen since I left Guatemala.

Note: These groups of drug traffickers call themselves the owners of the desert. Nobody can enter there without paying for their life.

After a while, the little boy who came with us was crying relentlessly because he was sick. The coyotes told his mother to shut him up, and if she did not shut him up, they would kill him and her. We were very angry because it would mean the death of another person, another life that they had no right to take. Shortly after, the child started feeling better and finally stopped crying. I kept thinking about how we had been in the desert for a long time and that one of us would soon die of dehydration. All the water was gone. We did not have anything left.

When I was in the desert, the cold and the sound left me with chills all over my body. On our journey, we saw the bones of all those people who died trying to cross. There were even some skulls under thorn bushes. It was horrifying to see.

Note: The desert is like a cemetery of dreamers who were not able to arrive to their destination or reach their goal.

Things were getting worse, and we were still in the desert. We could not walk anymore. People started to complain to the coyotes asking why they had lied to us.

They turned to us and said, "That's the American Dream. You have to suffer in order to get it." Back when we were in Mexico, the coyotes had told us that we would be arriving very soon to the United States, and everyone remained silent.

We had to rest for a while under the bushes. The coyotes started to get high and were unconscious. A coyote approached me, he spoke to me in Spanish, and I answered him in my native language. The other coyotes still thought I did not speak Spanish and told him to leave me alone. They called me illiterate, but I understood them perfectly. I never tried to defend myself. After that, they started to touch a girl that I think was barely eighteen years old. They dragged her and raped her. She pleaded for them not to hurt her, but no matter what she said, they would not stop.

Note: Not being able to help someone for fear of getting hurt becomes remorse that will forever live inside you and will never let you live in peace.

Nobody had done anything to stop them because they were well armed. Some of the men started to fight with the coyotes, and the fight was becoming very violent. Without anyone realizing it, a group of the US border patrol came out, and everyone started to run, but it was impossible to escape. Out of nowhere, the coyotes disappeared, and they disappeared without us.

The US border patrol arrested us, put us in white vans, and took us to an immigration detention center. Once we got there. The majority of border patrol were cruel to us. They would call us illegal and hit us for entering the country illegally. They treated us like animals by putting us in cages or a cold room that felt like a freezer. They would put us in rooms that were freezing for three days and tell us that we could leave if we signed their paper. They tried convincing us that it was a paper to leave the room when in reality, it was us signing for our own deportation.

Note: The sad reality is that not all border patrol agents are good. Some of them called us illegal, and sometimes they beat us like an animals for illegally entering in their country.

They were convinced that this treatment was the way we would learn to not come to this country. A lot of Central American men died by the hands of ICE when arrested at the border of the United States. A lot of men are beaten and tased at the immigration centers. Once we get there, they separate us by age and sex. Many people who bring their children are separated from them. ICE doesn't care if the children are crying or begging them to not separate them from their fathers.

After a few hours, ICE started asking us one by one for our information. They approached me and began to ask me question about where I had come from. When I responded in Spanish, the mom of the little boy was confused.

She asked me, "You speak Spanish?"

I told her, "I speak Spanish! Out of fear of the coyotes, I never spoke in Spanish with anyone because I did not want them to know that I could both speak and understand them.

She told me, "It was better that you didn't speak Spanish for your safety!"

If I had spoken in Spanish, the same thing that happened to the other poor girl would have happened to me.

Before they separated us, I told her that I wished her luck and that I hoped her son would get well especially after everything we had gone through in the desert. We said goodbye and never saw each other again. I was in immigration custody but was released because

I was a minor. They sent me to an orphanage in Houston, Texas, where I lived for two months.

My mother was very worried about me. She thought I was dead. I finally called Guatemala three months later. Once I called, the first thing I asked for was my son. My mom told me that he was fine and that calmed me down. I told my mom, "I'm here, Mom. I achieved it!"

My mom said, "*God* has heard my prayers!"

I couldn't help but shout gratefully about how *God* had helped me in this struggle! I knew he was with me every step of the way. That was when she asked me if I had found my father.

Through many apologies, I told her that I did not know anything about him yet. I promised her that I would look for him until I knew where he was.

"I know you will, my daughter. I believe in you!" she said quietly.

I said goodbye to my mom and hung up the phone. I found myself on the streets with no family, no ability to speak English, and not even a penny in my wallet. All I knew was that I had to find somewhere to sleep.

Note: The majority of immigrants who leave to the United States do not have a family. These people have no choice but to sleep on the street. Still, however, there are Hispanics who are good people and are willing to provide a home.

After looking for a few hours, I didn't find anything and had to sleep on the street. The next day, a woman approached me and spoke to me in Spanish.

She asked if I was okay. What a question! Of course, I wasn't okay. I had slept on the street! So I turned to her slowly and replied by saying, "No. I had to sleep on the street, and I'm alone." The woman took me to her house and I told her everything that had happened. She decided to help by giving me a home, helping me find a job, and most importantly, helping me find my father.

Once I started working, I was happy because I could help my mother and my grandmother—my whole family. Two months had passed when I finally found my father. He had been hospitalized in McAllen, Texas.

The border patrol had found him half dead in the desert with signs of beatings. He was in rehab for the damages he suffered. He still had not woken up.

I begged the woman with whom I lived to help me go and see my father. She did not deny me the opportunity and helped me go. When I saw my father after almost a year, I started crying. The doctors let me see him in intensive therapy.

I was happy to see him but sad that he was lying in a hospital bed in a coma. I said to him, "Please, Dad, fight for your life! I came here to look for you, and I finally found you. Please fight for your life. Do not leave us!"

Note: God always listens to your prayers. When you believe that everything is possible, anything can happen. Faith moves mountains.

I quickly called my mother and declared through the phone that I had fulfilled my promise! I had found my father! My mom was excited at my news and thanked me while telling me that I was the best daughter in the world! I couldn't help but thank her for not abandoning me in these moments where I felt most alone.

After a few weeks, my father had regained consciousness. When he saw me, he immediately thought we were in Guatemala. I said, "Calm down, Daddy. We are in America! I am proud of you for having fought for your life, and I love you so much."

Every day when it dawns, my father tells me how proud he is of me because I risked everything in order to find him. He told me that when he is no longer in this world, he will always love me until the last day of his life.

Then we went to Houston, Texas, and called my family. The most important thing for me, however, was to talk to my son and hear that he was fine even though I was far away. I left him so that he would be safe. To this day, I prefer that my son is far from me than to have brought him and have had something happened to him.

A few months later, my grandmother died of diabetes, and I felt miserable. After a while, I stopped blaming myself and realized that it was not my fault. Even with everything that happened, life still made sense. As one day I promised her to go ahead, at this time, I'm struggling for my dreams and fulfilling my promises. Right now, I get to talk about the story of my life without fear of anything, or anyone. I know that in this world, we are only passengers.

My mother now has diabetes, and I will never let her suffer as my grandmother did. My mother will never lack medicine, and we will never deny her the medical attention she needs. My father and I will always carry pain in our hearts because we could not give my grandmother the adequate medical care she needed. All this was due to the circumstances in which we were living before.

I'm now in the United States fighting for my son and my family. I enrolled in school and began to study so that I could become someone in life. I will never give up or let someone make me think of myself as anything but great. It has been hard for me to forget what happened on my journey. In fact, it is the biggest pain I have ever experienced in my life. This crossing has marked my life forever.

The pain I experienced is the reason I try to be a better person every day and why I have my head held high. I repeat this to myself often because it's what I had to endure and conquer in order reach my destiny and achieve *The American Dream*.

Note: No matter how long I've been here, I will never forget where I come from. This is true even if I live in this country, and I earn more money here than I would have in Guatemala. I still feel poor in my heart.

I'm from Guatemala, and now you know about me.

Who am I, and why I am here?

How many battles have I had to win to earn respect of others?

Even though I've had to go through all this, I've still had to win the respect of my family, my friends, my bosses, and even my coworkers.

I grew up in extreme poverty to the point of not having shoes or clothes. The clothes I owned had holes. Those holes would remain until I sewed them shut and put another piece of clothing on underneath. All this just so that the hole would no longer be noticeable.

I have little time here, but I'm learning many things. I've learned to accept myself and to never let anyone make me feel less than him or her. Crossing a desert is not for weak. You have to be brave to do it.

The poverty in Guatemala is huge, and it is what has forced many people to immigrate to the country of dreams that is the United States.

Many people come to the USA because this is the country of opportunities!

There is so much poverty in Guatemala because of the people that are just as corrupt as our government is. The government does not provide support to families that need it, and there is as much violence as there is crime. Our government never does anything to stop what is happening.

Since then, people have started to leave their homes and immigrate to other countries. It is the most painful decision that a person has to make. It's ironic because when you leave, you give up seeing your family for a long time, and yet people do it for the welfare of their families. All this, and yet you never know if you will make it to your destination. Sometimes there is a good ending, but other times, the story has a very cruel end.

I have heard many sad stories of people who left their homes. It was difficult because many people have disappeared in parts of Mexico or are kidnapped by drug traffickers and put into human trafficking. So many families never recover their relatives again.

Note: Many people died and are still dying in the desert of the United States. It can take months to years to figure out who those people were and where they came from.

What I experienced was better compared to others. There are people who arrive at their destination but with a very cruel past. A lot of people don't want to talk about how they got here. It's hard to think about those people who hurt and abused us. However, now this past is nothing but memories. Just memories. We are stronger than those people who try to offend us for the way that we got here. We know that those people are not strong enough to do what we did. They would never dare cross a desert like we did.

Now the desert and the cactus are nothing but scars on our bodies. Every immigrant that comes to America has an unfixable pain because of what we went through to get to the United States. We are immigrants, and we are proud to be it. We will never be ashamed of who we are. Those memories of the past that hurt me have already been forgotten. Little by little those scars have healed, but the experience we had in the desert will always affect my life.

Note: Gallons of water along with our tears stayed in the desert. We are finally being rewarded for all our suffering and have come far from where we were before.

God has been my source of strength in every path I had to take to get here and because of him, nothing ever happened to me. God was there during the most horrible moment of my life. However, that also means he was there when I needed him most. It's better to always trust God over people because unlike others, he never abandons you.

I lacked everything I needed when I was a child, but food was always available. It did not matter that all we had was herbs and water, at least I never missed the love of *God*. I am grateful for my family and especially grateful to God for my son. He is the greatest blessing he has given me in life. A child will always be a blessing in life. Value your children because there are people who would like to have them and cannot.

I am a high school student and wrote this book to let people know how we, immigrants, arrive in the United States. It is hard for us to make this decision and even harder to decide to leave our families behind. I have also written this so that when my son is older, he will understand why I left him in Guatemala. It was never easy for me to do, but I knew that I had to do it.

Note: We as immigrants walked without stopping, and in those rare moments when we looked behind us, we wanted so badly to turn around and go back to everything we left behind.

This was said by *the heart of a young immigrant mother*.

Nobody will ever make me feel bad by calling me a wetback. I'll always be proud to have this identity because I know that person who is a wetback is more valuable than those who try to offend us. To face dangerous things and keep going are only for brave people like us wetbacks. I'm one of those people who are proud to be a wetback. In fact, I am a very strong person spiritually.

It's supposed to be America, the country of freedom. I can't understand what's going on right now. Sometimes I wonder why there's so much racism in any part of the United States if we are equal into God's eyes.

Note: The worst thing someone can do is compare people based on their nationalities. Martin Luther King Jr., the great man who changed the history of America, is the person who gives us strength as immigrants to fight for our rights and equality. He taught us that we have the right to live in peace and be free in this country.

Current Day

This photo was taken the last time I was with my son and the last time I saw him. I am a Mayan. In Guatemala, various languages are spoken. In fact, there are at least twenty-five different Mayan languages. I speak three of the languages that originate from Guatemala and also speak Spanish and English. I am a single mother and that makes me stronger every day. I was born in Quiché, Guatemala. I was born on September 8, 1999, and am now nineteen years old. I arrived in the United States on August 5, 2017. I lived in Houston, Texas,

for a couple of months and then moved to Seattle, Washington. I'm working and studying, and although it is complicated to do both at the same time, it is entirely worth it. Every day, I fight for my dreams because God has given me the opportunity to move on. Now that I am doing everything I had intended to do, I can't help but feel incredibly proud of my accomplishments. My mother often repeats a certain phrase to me that is crafted from beautiful words. This phrase uplifts my spirit, and every dawn I usually repeat it to myself. "Fight for what you want. If you surrender, you will never see the result of your efforts!"

About the Author

Rosa Ajanel came from a poor family. She worked as a seamstress and farmer as her parents. She had a son when she was sixteen years old. At present, her son is three years old. She left Guatemala in 2017. She is a Mayan woman and speaks Mayan dialects. She is also Hispanic,

and she is proud to be it. Spanish is not her first language, but she learned it when she was eight years old. It's a blessing for her to speak Spanish. Her life was so hard until she met Yuan Bai. Her life had changed a lot. She is so grateful to her because she helped her overcome those bad memories of her journey. Yuan Bai will always be her guardian angel and her soul mate. Her grandmother, at present, rests in peace, but she will always remain alive in Rosa Ajanel.

CPSIA information can be obtained
at www.ICGtesting.com
Printed in the USA
BVHW020348140120
569392BV00025B/2570/P